Bully Bad

By Zack Hix

Bully
Copyright © 2013

All Rights Reserved.
No part of this book may be reproduced in any form without permission in writing from the author or publisher.

ISBN: 978-1-935256-37-3

BackDoor Books
PO Box 1652
Boone, NC 28607
(828) 406-0469
ledgepress.com
ledgepress@gmail.com

About the Author: Zack Hix

My name is Zack Hix, I am 17 years old and live in Simpsonville, SC. I love to draw and make cartoon characters and I have many books filled with characters that I have created. My mom and I started a business in 2010 called Good Boy Roy based on the characters I draw and hope we can some day make it into a cartoon series and a brand name known everywhere. Now they are on t-shirts. This is the first book I have drawn illustrations for, it was fun for me to do. I love to fish, mountain bike, UGA Football, baseball, my family (mom, dad, sister Kelsie and 4 dogs—Cruz, Poncho, Maxine and Deuce). Maxine is my girl.

Hi, I'm Zack.
Have you ever been bullied?

If you have, then we have something in common.
I have been bullied too.

Do you know what bullying is?

It can mean different things to different people. But, I will tell you what I think a bully is.

I think a bully is someone who puts other people down, or makes fun of them, or hurts them.

I think they do it to make themselves feel more important or to be funny.

Being bullied can be done in a lot of ways.
For example, it can be physical, like pushing or hitting.

Ouch !!!
Hurting someone is not ok.

Bullying can be using words that may hurt someone's feelings or make them feel bad.

That is what happened to me the most. Kids would say mean things about my tics.

Bullying can also be done with email or texting someone mean or threatening messages. Or saying something out loud that is not nice or hateful about someone else.

Bullying can be done by one person or several people.

I even think someone looking at you or staring at you in a mean way is bullying. Words don't even need to be said.

Being bullied by other kids started for me in the 6th grade.

Other kids started teasing me and making fun of me because I developed an illness called Tourette's. Tourettes's causes you to have Tics.

6th

Tics are movements or sounds that someone's body makes without them making it happen. The person can't control what their body does.

Tics for me were random, jerky, face, neck and arm movements. It was very difficult for me. I could not control what my body was doing.

The kids didn't understand what was going on, and they teased me, a lot.
Every day. That made me sad, AND angry.

All of the teasing, mean words and bullying made me very sad and depressed.

Depressed is when you feel sad, a lot. When have you ever been sad? Why?

Some days I could not even eat lunch because I was sad and crying. My teachers would call my mom and tell her I was crying, again.

What would you do if you saw someone being teased or bullied?

Would you help them or join in and tease them too?

I told my teachers and my parents.

I think you should tell an adult that you trust if you are being bullied. They will know what to do and help you.

A lot of days I came home and cried. Most mornings I didn't want to get out of bed and go to school because I knew I was going to be made fun of.

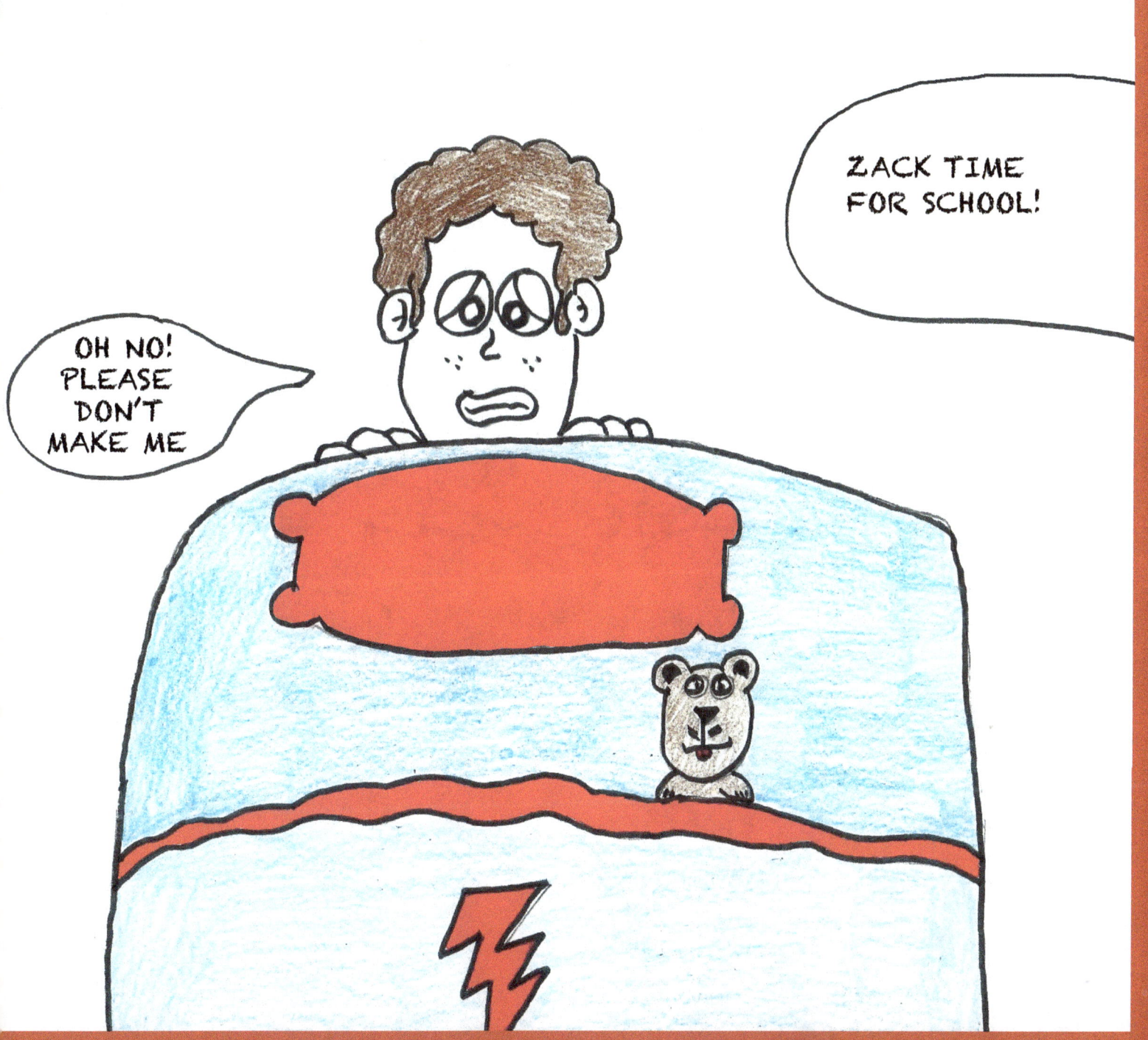

Just the idea of going into school and being made fun of would make me sad and scared.

That year, 6th grade, the teasing and bullying caused me to be so sad that I could not even finish school that year.

A teacher came to my house to teach me the lessons.

Did you know that 160,000 kids miss school each day for fear of bullying!
Wow! That's a lot. And, 1 in 10 drops out of school because of the bullying.

Have you ever been so sad or afraid that you didn't want to go to school?

Have YOU ever been mean to someone else?

STOP

THINK

THANK

RESPECT

Did you think about how it could make them feel?

Wouldn't it be great if we could all just get along?

Don't be a bully.

The End.

www.ingramcontent.com/pod-product-compliance
Lightning Source LLC
Chambersburg PA
CBHW081350040426
42450CB00015B/3381